HEAL ME, LORD

HEAL ME, LORD
An Ecumenical Prayerbook for Hospitals

Mary Brian Durkin, O.P.

FRANCISCAN HERALD PRESS
1434 West 51st Street • Chicago, Illinois 60609

HEAL ME, LORD: An Ecumenical Prayerbook for Hospitals
by Mary Brian Durkin, O.P. Copyright © 1987 by Franciscan
Herald Press, 1434 West 51st Street, Chicago, Illinois 60609.
All rights reserved.

Library of Congress Cataloging-in-Publication Data
Durkin, Mary Brian.
    Heal me, Lord.
        1. Sick—Prayer-books and devotions—English.
I. Title.
BV270.D87   1987   242'.86   87-8381
ISBN 0-8199-0911-4

ACKNOWLEDGEMENTS

The author and publisher gratefully acknowledge permission from
the following for the use of copyright material:

Central Conference of American Rabbis for excerpts from GATES
OF PRAYER, the New Union Prayerbook, copyright ©1975, Central
Conference of American Rabbis and Union of Liberal and Progres-
sive Synagogues.

Confraternity of Christian Doctrine, Inc. for excerpts from the NEW
AMERICAN BIBLE, copyright ©1970, Washington, D.C.

Doubleday & Company, Inc. for selected texts from THE JERUSA-
LEM BIBLE, copyright ©1966, Darton, Longman & Todd, Ltd. and
Doubleday & Company, Inc.

The Merton Legacy Trust, Anne H. McCormick, Administrator, for a
prayer by Thomas Merton in THOUGHTS IN SOLITUDE, Farrar,
Straus & Cudahy, copyright © 1958.

Paulist Press for a prayer by Edith Stein from the WRITINGS OF
EDITH STEIN, selected and translated by Hilda Graef, Peter Owen,
Ltd., London, copyright © 1956.

CONTENTS

PRAYERS IN TIMES OF SICKNESS AND PAIN

MORNING AND EVENING PRAYERS

O God, your goodness has brought me to the beginning
of a new day.
Will it bring suffering and anxiety or healing and renewed
strength?
Whatever it entails, pain or pleasure, joy or sorrow, I offer
it to you. Sanctify it so that each hour brings glory to you who
have watched over me during this illness. May the day bring
interludes of peaceful quiet when I can thank you for your
supportive love.

O God, who knows no darkness, watch over me tonight.
Grant to me and to all who are ill and distressed a
night of peaceful, healing rest. Bless my loved ones.
Protect all who labor here this night; bless them with
your gifts of health of mind, body and soul, as well
as joy and zeal in their work; for in ministering to
us, they serve you. All this I ask, Lord, confident of
your unfailing watchfulness.

A NIGHT PRAYER

Watch, O Lord,
with those who wake,
or watch,
or weep tonight,
and give your angels and saints
charge over those who sleep.
Care for your sick ones, O Christ,
Rest your weary ones;
bless your dying ones;
soothe your suffering ones;
comfort your afflicted ones;
shield your joyous ones—
all for your love's sake. Amen.

St. Augustine (354-430)

DURING ILLNESS

O GOD,
I beg you to give me the courage and patience
needed during this illness.
Help me to bear my pain and worry
without complaints;
sustain me when I become discouraged;
calm me when I am anxious.
Save me from grumbling and self-pity.
Help me to make these days of inactivity
a period of spiritual growth,
a time to grow closer to you
as you teach me courage, hope and love.
Divine Healer,
You are the giver of all good gifts:
bless me with your healing grace.

A PRAYER FOR RENEWED HEALTH

Lord, you promised never to forsake those
who truly love you; and so with confidence I come
to ask your help during these days of pain, worry
and separation from those I love.
When I am miserable, help me to remember
that you patiently endured suffering beyond measure
for my sake.
Comfort me with your presence and healing love.
When I am restless or irritable, help me
to recall your words: "My peace I give to you . . .
Do not let your hearts be troubled and do not be
afraid."
Centuries ago when you walked this earth,
you showed compassion on all who came to you;
I know that your power and love are as great today.
Do not refuse my plea: restore my health, so that
renewed in mind and body, soul and spirit,
I'll be able to return to my family and work,
to serve you ever more faithfully. This I ask
in your name, Jesus the Christ.

A PRAYER TO THE DIVINE PHYSICIAN

Dear Lord,
My whole body aches with pain!
I am anxious and confused by all that's happening to me.
My privacy and independence are being stripped away.
I'm not used to being told what I must do;
and to make it worse, no one answers my questions.
Forgive me if I seem irritable but I can't find any
meaning in this suffering.
How long will it go on?
Will I recover? Soon?

Yes, I'm worried and upset, yet I do trust you, Lord,
whatever your plans are for me. It's the not knowing
what is going to happen that frightens me. I worry
about the tests, treatments, medications, the prognosis,
the bills—everything!

Lord, grant me the grace to accept patiently these
days of pain, uncertainty, and worry.
Let them not be wasted by my complaints, distrust
and grumbling. You are the Divine Physician, the
true healer. Guide all those who are taking care of me.
Console me with the knowledge that I am in your hands.
Help me to be more trusting, more secure in your
compassionate, sustaining love.

Forgive my impatience, dear Lord. I truly trust in
your healing love.

IN TIME OF PAIN

Lord Jesus, sometimes I am so pain-wracked that I just cannot pray.
I trust that you are with me during those times; for you, too, knew pain, loneliness and anxiety. Yet, I do not always feel the comfort of your presence. When I find it difficult to pray, please
> help me to offer my suffering to our Father,
> as you brought your pain to him in Gethsemane;
> strengthen me with trusting love so that I may place myself in your Father's hands,
> as you did on the cross, when you said:
> "FATHER, into your hands I entrust my spirit."

A PRAYER FOR ACCEPTANCE

Dear Jesus,
You know what pain is.
You chose the cross as the way of salvation.
Those whom you invite to share the cross
are your special friends.

Help me to accept my suffering;
help me to bear it with you.
I give you my pain, my distress, my fears.
These are all I have to give while I am ill.

You were moved to pity—
    for the widow about to bury her only son,
    for the blind man, the cripple,
    for the lepers and a beggar.
You wept with the family of Lazarus.
You healed and comforted those in distress.

You know so well what weakness and suffering are.
In the Garden, you cried out:
    "Let this chalice pass . . ."
Give me, dear Lord, the strength and courage to say
with you:
    "Not my will but thine be done."

PRAYER OF A DISABLED PERSON

Loving Father,
help me to accept without bitterness this disability
which has suddenly altered my life.
Empower me to see beyond the limitations it imposes.
Teach me how to transform it into a blessing,
a means of deepening my trust in you.
Forgive my moments of frustration, anger, despondency.
Thank you for the lessons I am learning:
the need to treat everyone with dignity,
particularly those who have a disability: the stroke
victim, the blind, the mentally impaired, the paralyzed,
the fragile weak, all who are permanently injured.
Lord, I need to discipline myself
so that I can achieve whatever independence
is possible for me. I offer to you
the hours of therapy as a silent prayer
for all worn out with sickness and
wearied by pain; for all children, especially those
neglected, unloved, abused; and for the dying.
May they find peace with you. For myself,
I ask for the gift of patience, courage and
your compassionate love for all who suffer.

MINI-PRAYERS

Sometimes when you are ill, particularly when you are in pain or anxious, it is difficult to pray. Here is a simple but effective way to raise your heart and mind to God. Select from these names of Jesus Christ one or two titles that appeal to you. Say each one slowly to yourself, pondering its meaning. Your thoughts are a true prayer of praise and trust!

Jesus	Christ
The Good Shepherd	Our Rock
The Truth	Savior
The Light	Teacher
Prince of Peace	Physician
Lord of all	Divine Healer
Suffering Servant	Friend
The Word Made Flesh	Redeemer

FOR TIMES OF SICKNESS

Lord, teach me the art of patience while I am well;
and give me the use of it when I am sick. In that
day either lighten my burden or strengthen my back.
Make me, who so often in times of health have discovered
my weakness presuming on my own strength, to be strong
in my sickness when I rely solely on your assistance.

Thomas Fuller (1608-1661)

A PRAYER FOR COMPASSION

Show mercy to me, O Lord, who so often have been my
help, my strength. Pondering the situation of the
man who was held up by thieves, wounded and left
for half-dead as he was going down to Jericho, I
turn to you and beg you to be my Good Samaritan.
Take me up; help me . . . so that I can live to praise
you with renewed zeal.

St. Jerome C. 340-420

PRAYER BEFORE SURGERY

Creator Father, you know every fibre of my being. Graciously give your knowledge to the surgeon and all who assist in this operation. Inform their minds, guide their hands, steady their nerves.

As I am placed under the bright lights, may my fears be displaced by a sense of your presence as I say:
"Lord, I place my trust in you."

Bless my relatives, awaiting the outcome, with peace of mind and confidence in your providential care.

When the surgery is completed, may thoughts of the sufferings endured by Jesus Christ strengthen me to bear my pain without self-pity or complaints.

Loving Father, I beg you to answer my requests, not in proportion to my merits but in the bounty of your compassion.

AFTER SURGERY

Eternal Father, thank you for bringing me safely
through this operation and comforting me during those
first hours of recovery.
Forgive my fears and murmurings. Continue to heal me:
ease my pain, calm my mind, bless me with your courage
and patience.
I am grateful to you, and all who minister to my needs
in your name, for restoring me to health.
When I have regained my strength and am wholly healed,
I shall acknowledge your goodness to me by leading a
life that glorifies you, Father, and your Son, Jesus
the Christ.

WHILE KEEPING VIGIL . . .

O God, as I watch here at this bedside, I know that you hear my prayers that my dear one be restored to health. Help me during these hours of waiting and uncertainty. I'm so anxious that I don't even want to leave the room to eat or snatch some rest. Yet, I realize that I must take care of myself so that I am able to cope with whatever happens these next days.

I need your guidance and support, Lord. Help me to be sensible, to listen to those who are concerned about me during this vigil. You are my solace and strength; I rely on you to grace me with prudence as I wait for you to heal my loved one.

A PRAYER OF GRATITUDE

Jesus, when you suffered such agony in the garden before your death, you were consoled by your heavenly Father. During my illness, you have done the same for me. In my pain, anxiety and weakness, I felt your presence and was comforted by your promise: "Fear not, I am with you always." Each day has brought me reasons for gratefulness: pain lessened, anxiety relieved, health restored.

Thank you, Lord, for your healing gifts and for helping me to use the time of this illness wisely. I have felt your guidance as I used this enforced leisure time to reflect on the past and the future. I've put my priorities in order, faced some problems, rectified some situations. Each day I have grown closer to you. Your love has been visible in many intangible ways.

Lord, I thank you for all the graces given to me. May I live to be ever more worthy of your kindness.

ON RECOVERING FROM ILLNESS

I love the Lord because he has heard
my voice in supplication,
Because he has inclined his ear to me
the day I called.
Gracious is the Lord and just;
yes, our God is merciful.
The Lord keeps the little ones;
I was brought low and he saved me.
How shall I make a return to the Lord
for all the good he has done for me?
To you I will offer sacrifice of thanksgiving,
and I will call upon the name of the Lord.
My vows to the Lord I will pay
in the presence of all his people.

(Psalm 116)

DURING RECUPERATION

Dear God, I want to go home. Soon, please! I didn't mind being hospitalized when I was really ill; but now I'm restless, bored, anxious to return to my family and friends. Please help me to accept the fact that healing doesn't happen overnight. Just as my illness developed over a period of time, regaining my strength will take time, too. Help me to remember that when I'm impatient. I know that I should be grateful that I was here to receive restorative care; instead I'm complaining about not being released. Forgive me, Lord; bless me with patience.

A PRAYER FOR FORGIVENESS

Dear God,
for a long time I have separated myself from you.
At first, it was not deliberate. I drifted away,
neglecting prayers and going to church, too occupied,
too pressured to take time to acknowledge that you
are one to whom I owe devotion.
Now I feel that I have neglected you for so long
that it is presumptuous to ask your help. But when
I think of your forgiving love shown to so many:
the adulterous woman, cowardly Peter, the thief
on the cross, then I am not afraid to ask your
forgiveness.
Lord, pardon my indifference, my neglect, my
self-sufficiency that made me act as though I
did not need your help.
Forgive me, Lord. Heal me.
Restore, renew and re-vitalize my love for you,
the giver of peace and joy, of health, body and mind.
I am yours, Lord.
Make me yours.

PRAYER FOR PEACE, COURAGE, SERENITY

Let nothing disturb you.
Let nothing dismay you:
All things pass;
God never changes.
Patience attains
All that it strives for.
Any one who has God
Finds nothing is lacking:
God alone suffices.

St. Teresa of Avila (1515-1582)

PRAYER FOR PEACE, COURAGE, SERENITY

Send down, O God, O Gentle, O Compassionate
into my heart
FAITH,
TRANQUILITY,
STILLNESS,
that I may be one of those whose hearts
are tranquilized by the mention of God.

Muslim Prayer

Lord, I need only
one thing in this world:
to know myself and to love you.
Give me your love and your grace;
with these, I am rich enough
and desire nothing more.

Pope John XXIII (1881-1963)

A MOTHER'S PRAYER OF GRATITUDE

Loving Father of us all,
as I hold my new baby and marvel at the perfection
of curled fingers, tiny ears and half-smiling lips,
my heart zooms with happiness—and gratitude to you.

Did you feel a similar surge of joyous pride
when you first saw your very own creation:
sun and stars; sea and sky; the first man and woman?
As I hold this miracle of newness, I am overcome by
happiness, relief, thanksgiving, awe—and a little fear, too.
The world is so confused and chaotic; the responsibilities
of parents are so demanding and never lessening!
But I am not really afraid for I trust in your guidance.

You walked beside me, supporting and encouraging me
during those long months of waiting and wondering;
and I know that your loving care will be with me now
and in the years ahead.

Jesus the Christ was your gift to the world;
this precious child is your gift to my husband and me.
Bless us with the wisdom, patience and courage
to bring up our child to love and honor you
and your son, Jesus the Christ.
Bless and protect our little one, now and always.
You who are indeed the giver of all good gifts,
hear our song of gratitude for this gift of new life.

A MOTHER'S CRY FOR HER CHILD

God! I'm outraged at the loss of my baby.
For months I've waited, endured discomfort,
did everything I was supposed to do so that our
child would be healthy—all for nothing! Why
did it happen to me? Why not someone who never
wanted a child in the first place? I don't understand.
Am I to blame? Are you?

No! Though I'm crushed by this disappointment,
I believe that you *do not will* such calamities.
You want us to be healthy, whole, happy. But,
do you care when something like this happens?
Does my emptiness matter to you? And do you
understand why I cannot pray now? All I dare ask is
that, overlooking my bitterness, you will take care
of my baby the way I wanted to and comfort me
in the vacant hours ahead. Please, Lord, walk beside me.

A PRAYER TO OVERCOME ADDICTION

Dear God, help me to see the truth about my addiction.
I've been off balance for so long; now I want to get my life
in order. Help me. Help me to accept help. I've taken
the first step: I've ripped off the masks that I've been hiding
behind: the bluff that everything was the fault of others:
my folks, friends, the job, my fears, lost dreams—everything
was to blame, except me. Not true! I am to blame; help me,
Lord, to change. The most difficult thing is that when I
admit that I've failed myself, and those I love, I get so
dejected that I lose courage.

A chaplain told me to stop thinking of the past.
"You won't get better grovelling in guilt," he warned.
"The Lord loves you now but he loved you when you were
ruining your life, too. He loves us even when we are
sinners—so shove the guilt. Start over, but don't try
to do it alone."

The idea that you loved me, despite the past, has given
me some self-respect. Lord, strengthen me to accept
help and healing from you and those who minister in
your name. And if I think of giving up anytime during
the program, stretch out your hand to help me as you
did to Peter when he was sinking under the waves. I rely
on your saving help now and each day to come. "Help
me, Lord, that I may be healed. Save me that I may be
saved."

IN TIMES OF DISCOURAGEMENT

The Lord spoke: "I shall look for the lost one,
bring back the stray, bandage the wounded and make the
weak strong."

—Ezekiel 34:16

TO GOD OUR LIFE-GIVER

God of life,
there are days when the burdens we carry
weary us and wear us down;
when the road seems dreary and endless,
the skies gray and threatening;
when our lives have no music in them,
and our hearts are lonely;
our courage and trust falter.
Flood our way with light,
we beg you;
turn our eyes where the skies are
full of promise for a better day.

Saint Augustine (354-430)

A PRAYER TO JESUS, OUR HEALER

Jesus,
in time of weakness,
   be my strength;
in time of desolation,
   be my consolation;
in time of loneliness,
   be my companion;
in time of doubt,
   be my security;
in time of weariness,
   be my rest;
in sickness of mind, body or soul,
   be my Healer.

A PRAYER FOR PEACE AND UNITY

Eternal Father,
We pray for all on this earth,
though divided into nations and races,
yet all are your children,
drawing from you their life and being,
commanded by you to obey your laws,
each in accordance with the power
to know and understand them.
We ask you to cause hatred and strife to vanish
so that abiding peace may fill the earth,
and humanity everywhere may be blessed with your peace.
Then shall the spirit of brotherhood and sisterly love
show to the world a sincere faith
that you are Father of all.

From the Liberal Jewish Prayer Book

PRAYERS FOR THE DYING, THE DEPARTED AND THOSE WHO MOURN

PRAYER FOR A HAPPY DEATH

O Lord, support us
all the day long of this troublesome life,
until the shadows lengthen, the evening comes
and the busy world is hushed;
the fever of life is over
and our work is done.

Then Lord, in thy great mercy,
grant us a safe lodging,
a holy rest
and peace at the last,
through Jesus Christ, Our Lord. Amen.

Cardinal Newman (1801-1890)

A PRAYER FOR THE SICK AND DYING

O Lord Jesus Christ,
who in your last agony did commend your spirit into
the hands of your heavenly Father, have mercy on the
sick and dying.
May death be for them the gate to everlasting life;
in their last hours of this life fortify them with
the assurance of your presence even in the dark valley.
All this we ask in your name, for you are the resurrection
and the life, to whom glory and praise are due, forever
and ever.

Adapted from the Sarum Primer

A PRAYER FOR THE DEPARTED

Remember, O Lord, the souls of your servants
who have gone before us with the sign of faith, and
now slumber and sleep in peace. We beseech you, O Lord
to graciously grant to them and all who rest in Christ,
a place of refreshment, light and peace, through Christ
our Lord.

The Roman Canon

O God, full of compassion, eternal spirit of the universe, grant perfect rest under the wings of your presence to our loved one who has entered eternity. Master of mercy, let him (her) find refuge forever in the shadow of your wings and let his (her) soul be bound up in the bond of eternal life. The eternal God is his (her) inheritance. May he (she) rest in peace.

O Lord, healer of the brokenhearted and binder of their wounds, grant consolation to those who mourn. Give them strength and courage in the time of their grief, and restore to them a sense of life's goodness.

Fill them with reverence and love for you, that they may serve you with a whole heart and let them soon know peace.

Gates of Prayer

A PRAYER FOR ETERNAL PEACE
AND HAPPINESS

Receive, Lord, in tranquility and peace,
the soul of your servant who has left this earthly life
to be with you. Give our beloved one the life
that knows no age, the good things that do not pass away
through Jesus Christ our Lord.

Ignatius Loyola (1491-1556)

A PRAYER FOR THE SORROWING

O Lord,
who healed the broken-hearted
and bound up their wounds,
grant your consolation to all who mourn.
Strengthen and support them and all whom they love;
grant them a long and good life.
Put into their hearts a sincere love of you
so that they may serve you with a perfect heart.

Jewish Authorized Daily Prayer Book

A PRAYER FOR LETTING GO

We seem to give them back to you, O God, who gave them to us. Yet, just as you did not lose them in giving; so we do not really lose them when they return to you. For you give, not as the world gives, O Lord. What you give, you do not take away; and what is yours is ours also if we belong to you.

Help us to realize that life is eternal and love is immortal, that death is only an horizon, and an horizon is nothing save the limit of our sight. Lift us up, O strong Son of God, that we may see further; cleanse our eyes that we may see more clearly; draw us closer to you that we may know ourselves, to be nearer to our beloved ones who are now with you. And while you prepare a place for us, prepare us also for that happy place, that where you are, we may also be for evermore.

Bede Jarrett, OP (1881-1934)

FOR ALL SUFFERERS

Watch, O Lord, all those who wake or watch or weep tonight, and give your angels charge over those who sleep. Tend your sick, O Lord Christ; rest your weary; bless the dying; soothe all who suffer; shield all who love you.

St. Augustine (354-430)

A PRAYER FOR THOSE WHO SUFFER

O Lord God, we beg you to regard with divine pity, the pains of all your children. Grant that the passion of our Lord and his infinite merits may make fruitful for good the sufferings of the sick and the sorrows of the bereaved. This we ask in the name of him who suffered in our flesh and died for our sake, your Son and our Savior Jesus Christ.

Scottish Book of Common Prayer

I acknowledge, O Lord my God and God of my fathers, that both my cure and my death are in your hands. May it be your will to send me perfect healing. Yet if my death be fully determined by you, I will in love accept it at your hands . . .

You are the father of the fatherless and judge of the widow; protect my beloved kindred with whose soul my own is knit. Into your hands I commend my spirit. Amen, and Amen.

The Hebrew Prayer Book

(The following is added when death is imminent)

The Lord reigneth; the Lord hath reigned; the Lord shall reign for ever and ever.
Blessed be his name, whose glorious kingdom is for ever and ever.
The Lord, he is God.
Hear, O Israel, the Lord our God, the Lord is one.

The Hebrew Prayer Book

A HYMN OF PRAISE

Acclaim Yahweh, all the earth,
Serve Jahweh gladly,
come into his presence with songs of joy!

Know that he, Jahweh, is God,
he made us and we belong to him,
we are his people, the flock that he pastures.

Walk through his porticoes giving thanks,
enter his courts praising him,
give thanks to him, bless his name!

Yes, Yahweh is good,
his love is everlasting,
his faithfulness endures from age to age.

(Psalm 100)

A PRAYER TO INSTILL CONFIDENCE

"Out of his infinite glory,
may he give you the power through his Spirit
for your hidden self to grow strong,
so that Christ may live in your hearts
through faith, and then,
planted in love and built on love,
you will with all the saints have strength
to grasp the breadth and the length,
the height and the depth;
until, knowing the love of Christ,
which is beyond all knowledge,
you are filled with the utter fullness of God."

(Ephesian 3:16-19)

COMFORTING, INSPIRING
THOUGHTS

Cast all your cares on him because he cares for you

(1 Peter 5:7)

Heal me, O Lord, that I may be healed; save me that I may be saved; for it is you whom I praise.

(Jeremiah 17:14)

"Eye has not seen, ear has not heard,
nor has it so much as dawned on man
what God has prepared for those who love him."

(1 Corinthians 2:9)

Create in me a clean heart, O God, and
put a new and right spirit within me. . . .
A broken and contrite heart, O God, you will
not despise.

(Psalm 51: 12.19)

Come to me all you who labor and are overburdened
and I will give you rest. Shoulder my yoke and learn from me
for I am gentle and humble in heart, and you will find rest
for your souls. Yes my yoke is easy and my burden light.

(Matthew 11: 28-30)

By the might of his glory you will be endowed with the
strength needed to stand fast, even to endure joyfully
whatever may come.

(Colossians 1:11)

Though a person be soiled
With the sins of a lifetime,
Let that person love me
with sincerity and true devotion:
I see no sinner—
I see a holy person
Loved by me.

The Bhagavad-Gita, Hindu

Even if I have gone astray, I am still your child,
O God. You are my mother and father.

Arjan - 1606 - Guru Sikh

At last I admitted to you that I had sinned,
no longer concealing my guilt.
I said: "I will go to Yahweh
and confess my fault."
And you, you have forgiven the wrong I did,
have pardoned my sin.

(Psalm 32:5)

Life is no less beautiful
when it is accompanied
by illness or weakness,
hunger or poverty,
physical or mental ill health,
loneliness or old age.

Terence Cardinal Cooke (1921-1983)

Fear not, I am with you; be not dismayed; I am your
God. I will strengthen you and help you, and uphold you
with my right hand of justice.

(Isaiah 41:10)

Then you can invoke me in your troubles
and I will rescue you, and you shall honor me.

(Psalm 50:15)

Praised be the God and Father of our Lord Jesus Christ,
a gentle Father and the God of all consolation, who
comforts us in all our sorrows, so that we can
offer others in their sorrow the consolation
that we have received from God ourselves.

(2 Corinthians 1:3.4)

Yes, the troubles which are soon over, though
they weigh little, train us for the carrying of a weight of
eternal glory which is out of all proportions to them.

(2 Corinthians 4:17)

Do not be afraid, for I have redeemed you;
I have called you by your name, you are mine. . . .
Should you walk through fire, you will not be scorched;
and the flames will not burn you.

(Isaiah 43:1.3)

Can a mother forget her infant . . . ?
Even should she forget
I will never forget you.
See, upon the palms of my hands I have written your name.

(Isaiah 49:15-16)

TRUST

I have an ever deeper and firmer belief
that nothing is merely an accident
when seen in the light of God—
that my whole life, down to the smallest details,
has been marked out for me in the plan
of Divine Providence and has a completely
coherent meaning in God's all-seeing eyes.

Edith Stein (1891-1942)

I believe in the sun even when it
   is not shining;
I believe in love, even when
   I feel it not;
I believe in GOD, even when
   he is silent.

Words written on the wall of a cellar in
Cologne, Germany, after World War II.

TRADITIONAL PRAYERS

THE LORD'S PRAYER

Our Father, who art in heaven,
hallowed be thy name;
thy kingdom come;
thy will be done on earth as it is in heaven.
Give us this day our daily bread;
and forgive us our trespasses,
as we forgive those who trespass against us;
and lead us not into temptation,
but deliver us from evil.
Amen.

THE HAIL MARY

Hail Mary, full of grace,
the Lord is with thee.
Blessed art thou among women,
and blessed is the fruit of thy womb, Jesus.
Holy Mary, Mother of God,
pray for us sinners, now,
and at the hour of our death.
Amen.

THE DOXOLOGY

Glory to the Father,
and to the Son,
and to the Holy Spirit,
as it was in the beginning,
is now, and ever shall be,
world without end, Amen.

THE APOSTLES' CREED

I believe in God the Father Almighty, Creator of
heaven and earth; and in Jesus Christ, his only Son, our Lord,
who was conceived by the Holy Spirit, born of the
Virgin Mary, suffered under Pontius Pilate, was crucified,
died and was buried; he descended into hell; the third
day he rose again from the dead; he ascended into heaven,
sits at the right hand of God the Father Almighty; from
thence he shall come to judge the living and the dead.
I believe in the Holy Spirit, the Holy Catholic Church; the
communion of saints, the forgiveness of sins, and
life everlasting. Amen.

THE MEMORARE

Remember,
O most gracious virgin Mary,
that never was it known that anyone
who fled to your protection,
implored your help,
and sought your intercession,
was left unaided.
Inspired with this confidence,
I fly to you,
O Virgin of Virgins, my mother.
To you I come, before you I stand,
sinful and sorrowful.
O mother of the Word Incarnate,
Despise not my petitions, but in your mercy
hear and answer me. Amen.

SHORT PRAYERS OF FAITH, HOPE, LOVE AND CONTRITION

O God, I firmly believe all the truths that you have revealed and that you teach through your Church, for you are truth itself.

O God, relying on your infinite power, goodness and mercy, I hope with complete trust that, through the merits of Jesus Christ, you will pardon my sins and grant me the grace to serve you faithfully in this world so as to merit eternal happiness in the next.

O God, I love you with my whole heart above all things, because you are infinitely good. For your sake, I love my neighbor as I love myself. Help me, Lord, to keep your great commandment: "Love one another, as I have loved you."

O God, I am sorry for all my sins because you are goodness itself and sin is an offense against you. Therefore I firmly resolve, with the help of your grace, to avoid sin and all occasions of temptation.

A PRAYER BEFORE COMMUNION

Lord, Jesus Christ, I have approached your altar
many times to receive you. Now, during my illness,
you graciously come to me. May the grace of this
Communion sustain me.
Eternal Physician, in your compassion,
restore my health,
ease my pain and worries.
Yet, if these blessings are not in your immediate plans
for me, then I ask you to strengthen me to accept
whatever is to be.
You, Lord, are my hope, my peace, my friend.
Thank you for coming to me.

A PRAYER AFTER COMMUNION

Lord, I thank you for coming to me.
May your presence encourage, strengthen and comfort
me throughout this day.
Fill me with your peace and love.
Heal me, body and soul,
so that restored to health, I may return home,
there to serve you more faithfully.
For the gift of yourself, I can only say:
"Thank you, Lord, thank you."

AN ACT OF SPIRITUAL COMMUNION

Lord, I believe that you are truly present in this sacrament.
I sincerely wish that I could receive you now, but since I
am not able to do so, come spiritually into my heart. I unite
myself to you. Never permit me to be separated from you,
my Lord and my God.

St. Alphonsus (1696-1787)

PRAYER OF ST. FRANCIS

Lord, Make me an instrument of your peace.
 Where there is hatred,
 let me sow love;
 where there is injury, pardon;
 where there is doubt, faith;
 where there is darkness, light
 and where there is sadness, joy.

O Divine Master, grant that I may
 not so much
 seek to be consoled as to console;
 to be understood as to understand;
 to be loved as to love.
 For it is in giving that we receive;
 it is in pardoning that we are pardoned;
 and it is in dying that we are born
 to eternal life.

A REMINDER: GOD HAS A PLAN

God has created me to do him some definite service;
He has committed some work to me which
he has not committed to another.
I have my mission . . . .
I am a link in a chain,
a bond of connection between persons.
God has not created me without a reason.
I shall do good;
I shall do his work.
Therefore, I will trust him.
Whatever, wherever I am,
I am always useful.
When I am in sickness, my sickness may serve him;
if I am in sorrow, my sorrow may serve him.
God does nothing in vain.
He knows what he has in mind for me.
I trust my God, my creator, my redeemer.

Cardinal Newman (1801-1890)

A PRAYER OF TRUST IN GOD'S PROVIDENCE

My Lord God,
I have no idea where I am going.
I do not see the road ahead of me.
I cannot know for certain where it will end.
Nor do I really know myself,
and the fact that I think that I am following
your will does not mean that I am actually doing so.
But I believe that the desire to please you
does in fact please you.
And I hope I have that desire in all that I am doing.
I hope that I will never do anything apart from
that desire.
And I know that if I do this,
you will lead me by the right road though I may
know nothing about it.
Therefore will I trust you always though I may seen
lost and in the shadow of death.
I will not fear, for you are ever with me,
and you will never leave me to face my peril alone.

Thomas Merton (1915-1968)

PSALM 23

The Lord is my shepherd; I shall not want.
In verdant pastures he gives me repose;
Beside restful waters he leads me;
he refreshes my soul.
He guides me in right paths
for his name's sake.

Even though I walk in the dark valley
I fear no evil; for you are at my side
With your rod and your staff
that give me courage.

You spread the table before me
in the sight of my foes;
You anoint my head with oil;
my cup overflows.
Only goodness and kindness follow me
all the days of my life;
And I shall dwell in the house of the Lord
for years to come.

A HEALTHY PHILOSOPHY

You should live in accord with the spirit. . . .
The fruit of the spirit is love, joy, peace, patient endurance,
kindness, generosity, faith, mildness and chastity. . . . Let us
not grow weary in doing good; if we do not relax our
efforts, in due time we shall reap our harvest.

(Galatians 5: 16. 22-23; 6:9-10)